The Painless F
PROPER ENGLISℍ ⌣⌣⌣⌣⌣

MW00979458

PROF. PERRY'S
POPULAR PEDAGOGICAL PICTORIALS
Proudly Presents

The Painless Path to
PROPER ENGLISH USAGE

Ably Arranged, Edited and Illustrated by

Stan Malotte

St. Martin's Press
New York

Library of Congress Cataloging-in-Publication Data

Malotte, Stan.

   The painless path to proper English usage.

   1. English language—Usage—Dictionaries.
2. English language—Usage—Caricatures and cartoons.
I. Title.
PE1460.M278 1987   428.3   87-4469
ISBN 0-312-00714-0

Originally published by R. & E. Miles, San Pedro, CA.

Names herein are fictional. Any resemblance to real persons or products is unintentional.

USER'S NOTE

 Because the word pairs are arranged alphabetically by only the first word, a complete index is included. Further help also appears: Appendix A reprints an old rhyme on the parts of speech, and Appendix B gives a sample listing of American vs. British spellings, a continuing source of confusion for us all.

For Shirley

Preface

For his book, Prof. Perry has chosen 126 of the most frequently confused words in our language. Most are included in the usage chapters of our standard high school and college texts. Despite our schools' best efforts, however, we still see examples of mis-usage in the media and daily business communications — and, even worse, do not see them as they sneak by in our own writing.

To straighten us all out, Prof. Perry first explains the correct usage for each word and then farther clarifi . . . oops! . . . *further* clarifies the lesson with examples from his personal collection of rare grammatical art. These magnificent illustrations, incidentally, have been hanged in some of . . . excuse me . . . have been *hung* in some of the principle . . . I mean *principal* . . . well, it's obviously time we get started.

— S.M.

The Painless Path to
PROPER ENGLISH USAGE

accept/except

Use **accept** to mean *receive*. Just think of other words that begin with *ac* and also have a sense of *receiving* — like *ac*quire and *ac*cumulate. (The prefix *ac* is from the Latin and means *toward*.) **except** means *not included*. Its first two letters (*ex*) are the Latin prefix that means *from*, as in *ex*cerpt, *ex*tract, and other *ex* words suggesting *to take from*.

affect / effect

affect (*to have an influence on*) is always a verb,* as in "Too much
rain will **affect** plant growth adversely." **effect** is usually a noun, as in
"The right amount of rain has a good **effect** on plant growth." However,
effect can also be a verb meaning to *bring about a result*, as in "The
right amount of rain will help **effect** [*bring about*] proper plant
growth." The principal thing to remember is that **affect** is always a
verb — its a stands for action.

*Except for its special use in psychology.

aggravate/annoy

aggravate is commonly misused to mean *annoy*. We can **annoy** people and we can **aggravate** (*increase the unpleasantness of*) an already unpleasant effect or situation, but we cannot "aggravate" people. That would mean we would "increase" them.

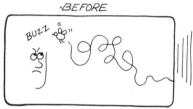

15

all ready / already

all ready means that *everything is prepared, all is ready.* **already** (an adverb) refers to *time,* as in "Are you here **already**?" (*so soon?*), "We did that **already**!" (*previously!*), etc.

all right/"alright"

all right is the correct word. **"alright"** is a nonstandard version of **all right** and is not to be written by users of this book.

all together/altogether

The meanings are altogether different. **all together** means the individual items are *not separated*, they are together. **altogether** means *totally*, *entirely*, as in "**Altogether** there were 14 deer at the river **all together** at one time."

Chapter 4: Bill Was Usually Right
From: The Life of Bill the Foreman
I'M NOT ALTOGETHER CONVINCED WE HAVE THE SHIP ALL TOGETHER YET, SIR.
X HERE
TOO LATE!
RIGHT AGAIN, BILL.
ACE SHIPYARDS

amount/number
fewer/less

amount refers to volume or bulk. **number** refers to separate items you can count. For instance, you can't count rain, but you can count raindrops (although you must hurry). The same logic applies to **fewer** and **less**. You would *not*, for example, say, "We had fewer rain this year." You would say, "We had **less** rain — and therefore **fewer** raindrops."

any body / anybody
any more / anymore
any one / anyone
any time / anytime
any way / anyway

As two separate words, each of these reveals its meaning in the second part. For example, the separate **more** in **any more** indicates the subject under discussion is **more**, whereas in the combined **anymore**, the emphasis is shared equally by both parts, thus forming a brand new word. Just analyze the meaning you want to get across. The same logic applies to compound words like *everybody, everyday,* and so on.

ERRORS TO AVOID #186

In this example, the detective has properly called everyone into the library but has made the common mistake of providing large quantities of chocolates for the suspects. This tends to elicit irrelevant comments and delay the investigation. Normally, only small quantities of chocolates should be provided.

apt / liable / likely

apt (from the same root as *aptitude*) suggests *proneness, natural tendency.*
liable means *subject to, susceptible.* **likely** suggests *probability.*

Weather Bureau Wins Award

Excitement reigned all over the weather bureau this week when forecasters there won the coveted "Good English Usage in Meteorology Award."

"Four statements especially stand out," said Willard Kookyboodle, president of the American Award Giving Society, a private group that travels about the country giving awards. The four statements have been permanently engraved on a plaque that will serve as a durable reminder of the words actually spoken. "Sound fades," explained Mr. Kookyboodle during

AAGS GEUIM AWARD WINNERS

1. IT VERY **LIKELY** WILL RAIN, MAYBE.
2. THIS AREA IS **LIABLE** TO RAIN AND OTHER FORMS OF WEATHER.
3. IF IT RAINS TOO MUCH, THE STREETS ARE **APT** TO FLOOD.
4. HEAD FOR THE HILLS!

FORECASTERS view award plaque engraved with Bureau's winning weather report statements.

27

assure / ensure / insure / reassure

assure means *to help remove doubt, to bolster confidence.* **ensure** means *to make certain of something.* Use **insure** only for *commercial insurance* purposes. **reassure** means *to give further encouragement, to restore confidence.* (NOTE: In British usage, *assure* is used for the commercial insurance sense.)

THE ADVENTURES OF BILL THE BUTLER
I ASSURE YOU, MADAME, IT WILL ARRIVE.
BUT HOW DO WE KNOW?! WHAT DID YOU DO TO ENSURE ITS ARRIVAL?
TO ENSURE ITS ARRIVAL, MADAME, I INSURED IT.
PAR'N ME. I GOTTA PACKAGE.
ACE
OH, I FEEL SO UNSURE!
REASSURE HER, SIR, WOULD YOU?
SURE
IT'SA INSURED PACKAGE FOR A "MADAME LA BOUCHE"
THERE THERE
OH, CEASELESS INCERTITUDE!
PLEASE STOP BOTHERING US!

a while/awhile

while is a noun and nouns are used with prepositions like *for*. So, we say, "Let's rest for **a while**." Putting **a** and **while** together makes the adverb **awhile**. Adverbs aren't used with prepositions; adverbs modify verbs. So, there's no need for the *for*. So, we say, "Let's rest **awhile**."

bad/badly

"I feel **bad**" (adjective) is the correct way to describe how you feel with, say, an *upset stomach*. "I feel **badly**" (adverb) means I have a *poor sense of touch* because adverbs tell how something is *done*. (NOTE: *feel* is a non-action verb. See also **good/well**.)

33

beside/besides

If you are **beside** (*next to*) someone and a third person joins you, there is now someone **besides** (*in addition to*) the two of you. He may also stand **beside** the two of you.

35

can/may

can means *is able to;* **may** indicates *permission.* Maybe this will help:
"I **can** can-can, but my doctor says I **may** not!"

LEADERSHIP SKILLS — Skill 8:
DECISION-MAKING

capital/capitol

Use **capital** for the city and **capitol** for the building.

censer/censor/censure

A **censer** is the small *container* in which incense is burned. **censor** means to *cut out objectionable material* (think of the o̲ in **cens̲o̲r** as standing for o̲ut). To **censure** is to *criticize* and *place blame*.

41

compare to/compare with

As a rule of thumb, use **compare to** to compare *in general;*
use **compare with** to compare *in detail*. Shakespeare, for example, wrote:
"Shall I **compare** thee **to** a summer's day?/Thou art more lovely and
more temperate." Had he written "Shall I **compare** thee **with** a summer's
day," he would have had to continue: "It begins at sunrise, you don't begin
until around 11; its temperatures are in the 80's whereas you have
cold hands," and so forth. Shakespeare knew how to use words.

43

complement / compliment

Use **complement** to mean *goes with, to make something more complete.*
Let the e̲ in comple̲ment remind you of the word *comple̲te.* A **compliment**
is something I̲ like to receive.

WHAT IS THIS MAN FORGETTING?*

*SCORE 10 points if you said "He's forgetting to tip his hat." Score only 8 points if you said "I don't know." (But add 2 points back on if you could have gotten the right answer if you had really thought about it.)

continual/continuous

Use **continual** for something that continues in an *off-and-on* manner (like **continual** barking). **continuous** means *non-stop*. Remember the difference by describing escaping steam as **continuousssssss**.

It was military history's saddest moment when Sgt. Bill was...

COURT-MARTIALED FOR OBEYING ORDERS

ORDERED TO KEEP A "CONTINUAL WATCH" OVER HIS AREA, SGT. BILL PERIODICALLY COVERED HIS EYES, THUS FOLLOWING ORDERS TO THE LETTER. HE WAS, NEVERTHELESS, COURT-MARTIALED, AND TODAY LIVES IN DISGRACE WITH HIS WIFE AND TWO LOVELY CHILDREN.

WHAT HIS SUPERIORS HAD MEANT TO SAY WAS: "KEEP A CONTINUOUS WATCH" OVER HIS AREA. THE DIFFERENCE IS SHOWN IN THE TWO PHOTOGRAPHS BELOW FROM THE NEWLY REVISED TRAINING MANUAL, *THE ADVENTURE OF GUARD DUTY.*

CONTINUAL
WATCH
NON-ALERT PHASE
(UNACCEPTABLE)

CONTINUOUS
WATCH
(MIL SPEC)

council/counsel/consul

council (noun) is a *group of people* who meet to discuss and decide things (e.g., the city **council**). **counsel** means *to give advice or guidance;* it also means the *advice given* (e.g., "The **counselor counseled** me and his **counsel** was good"). **consul** is *a person working in the foreign service* of his country. If you just remember the c̲ in **counc̲il** as relating to the c̲ity counc̲il, you'll have a head start.

desert / dessert

The verb **desert** (de·sert': *to abandon*) and the noun **desert** (des'ert: *arid land*) are both spelled with a single *s*. We can remember that the **dessert** we eat has *ss* because, of course, the *ss* stands for "*s*trawberry *s*hortcake."

IN THE OLD DAYS, PIONEER ANTS WOULD CROSS A VAST DESSERT LIKE THIS IN COVERED WAGONS.

HISTORY IS INTERESTING.

In 1849, when ants learned of a great DESERT that extended for hundreds of miles, they rushed west by the millions for what they thought would be the most glorious treat of their lives. Before they realized their mistake, they perished by the thousands. Once again, history shows the importance of good spelling. Because of this dramatic incident in their history, ants today are nearly all excellent spellers.

device/devise

device is the noun. **devise** is the verb. We **devise** a **device**. Just remember: the ability to **devise** something shows you're quite wise and the **device** you create is always quite nice.

disinterested/uninterested

Use **disinterested** to mean *impartial, neutral*. **uninterested** means you just don't care to hear about it — probably because it's <u>un</u>interesting.

OBSERVER RECOGNITION CHART REPLACES CHARTS 12 thru 84

DISINTERESTED OBSERVER

UNINTERESTED OBSERVER

STANDARD OBSERVER

PRO

CON

ZZZZ

emigrant/immigrant

When you permanently leave your country, you **emigrate** from that country (think of e̱ for e̱xit). When you come into your new country to stay, you **immigrate** (i̱ for i̱nto). Just remember that "e̱migrants e̱xit" and you'll have it.

WELL-KNOWN MYSTERIES SOLVED!

At what precise moment does the change occur from EMIGRANT to IMMIGRANT?* ❓ ❓

(E)MIGRANTS (E)XIT THE PLACE
WHERE THEY'VE BEEN,
GO (I)NTO SOME NEW PLACE AS
(I)MMIGRANTS THEN.

AS YOU CAN SEE, THEY'RE ALL
THE SAME BUNCH —
THEY DO IT, I THINK, TO GET
TWO TURNS AT LUNCH.

TYPICAL IMMIGRANT SHIP OF 1890
(WHERE DEEP INSIDE THE HULL) →

SHIP'S SALON

NOW, SAVE ROOM FOR 12:30

EMIGRANTS' LUNCH 11:30 – 12:30

IMMIGRANTS' LUNCH 12:30 – 1:30

I'M HAVING THE MEATLOAF AGAIN.

FORGET THE CHICKEN TODAY.

GRAZIE DANKE

I'M FULL

57

eminent/imminent

Use **eminent** for *well known, outstanding*. Use **imminent** for something that's *about to happen* <u>imm</u>ediately! (NOTE: *immanent* is a different word altogether and should be looked up for extra credit.)

every day / everyday

As two separate words, **every day** means *each separate day*. As one word, **everyday** means *ordinary, routine, commonplace*. We do **everyday** things practically **every day**.

UNCLE BILL'S

BRAIN TEASER #3: DICK'S DILEMMA

(A) DICK OWNS NICE SUITS FOR **EVERY DAY** OF THE WEEK. HE MUST WEAR THE SUIT DESIGNATED FOR THAT PARTICULAR DAY <u>ON</u> THAT PARTICULAR DAY!

(B) DICK ALSO OWNS AN ORDINARY EVERYDAY SUIT. HE MUST WEAR HIS **EVERYDAY** SUIT <u>EVERY DAY</u>!

(C) <u>PROBLEM:</u> HOW CAN DICK DO BOTH? (HINT: NO, HE CANNOT WEAR MORE THAN ONE SUIT AT A TIME.)

(D) <u>ANSWER:</u> IT CANNOT BE DONE.

61

farther/further

Use **farther** when referring to *physical distance*. Reserve **further** for all other uses such as "**further** in the future," "We'll discuss it no **further**," and so on. Think of the a in f<u>a</u>rther as standing for <u>a</u>rea.

THE STORY OF LITTER

EPISODE 12: BOGGED DOWN!

The FURTHER they investigated, the FARTHER they had to travel — till one day deep in the jungle...

Next Week: FURTHER DEVELOPMENTS!

flair/flare

If we can remember how to spell one of them, the other will take care of itself. Perhaps this will help: **flare** and *flame* are so close in meaning they differ by only one letter.

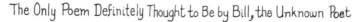

Alas! A Lass!

The Only Poem Definitely Thought to Be by Bill, the Unknown Poet

BILL

Alas! A lass who had no FLAIR
For knowing where to take her bear
To make folks stare and say, "Look there!"

Said "I know what!" and took a FLARE!

flaunt / flout

We are *show-offs* when we **flaunt** (*ostentatiously display*) and *rebels* when we **flout** (*openly defy*). Just remember "Bill's aunt who **flaunts** her independence by **flouting** the rules."

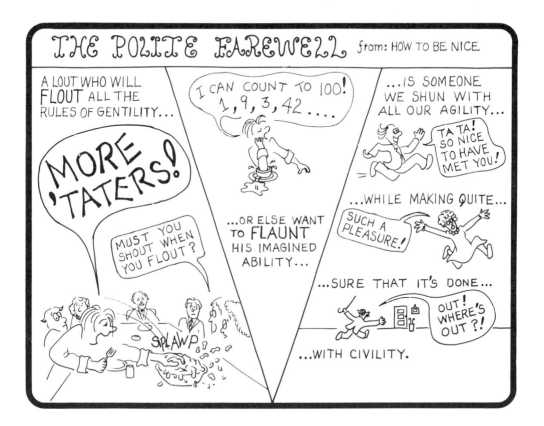

forbear/forebear

forbear means *to control oneself, to refrain from an impulse*. **forebear**, with an *e* in the middle, means *a relative from whom we are descended*. Just remember the connection with people who came be*fore* us. (NOTE: This logic should also help with *forgo* vs. *forego*.)

69

foreword/forward

You'll never confuse these two if you just remember that
the *word* that comes be*fore* is the **foreword.**

good/well

good is an adjective and therefore tells something about a noun, as in "She is a **good** singer." **well** is an adverb and therefore tells something about a verb — that is, how something is done — as in "She sings **well**." (NOTE: **good** can also be used with verbs, but *only with non-action verbs* like *looks*, *tastes*, and *feels*, as in "She sings **well** and *looks* **good**." We never say, "She sings good" or "The ice cream tastes well.")

73

hanged/hung

Both words are the past tense of *hang*, but **hung** is for pictures, **hanged** is for people.

75

I / me

I is the pronoun when *I* do something. **me** is used when something is done *to* me or *for* me, as in "He's done a lot for you and **me**" (*not* "for you and I"). **I** is the doer, **me** is the receiver.

The Hilarious Time Bill Couldn't Finish!

Now, some people say
(And I'll never know why):
"A gift came today
And it's for you and I!"

They really should jump
Up and down with great glee
And properly say
That it's "for you and ME!"

They never would say,
"Oh! This gift is for I!"
They'd say, "It's for ME!
If you touch it, you'll die!"

When "you" is there, though,
Something goes all awry —
They think they're polite
Saying "for you and I."

But it's wrong! Oh, 'tis wrong!
And should be corrected —
Along with "He don't"
And "She's fair complected,"

And other mistakes
Too num'rous to mention —
Which I'm going to anyway
So please pay ... oops! ...

imply / infer

imply means *to say something indirectly, to beat around the bush.*
infer means *to draw a conclusion* (perhaps from something that has
been **implied**).

79

in/into

Use **in** if something is *already inside*. Use **into** if it's *in the process of entering*. For example: "He decided he would not jump **into** the lake when he noticed that he was already **in** the lake."

THE AMAZING PHIL STARTLES SCIENCE!
THE VERY MOMENT AFTER I WALK INTO THAT ROOM, I WILL BE IN THAT ROOM!
ROOM
AMAZING
CAN HE DO IT?
AMAZING
I AM NOW IN THIS ROOM!
AMAZING!
AMAZING!
NOW, LET'S SEE—IF I WALK INTO THAT WALL...
AMAZIN

incredible / incredulous

Use **incredible** to mean *not to be believed* and **incredulous** to mean *skeptical.* Just remember the ending *–o-u-s* as in "<u>o-u-s</u> just pullin' my leg!"

83

ingenious/ingenuous

ingenious means *clever, inventive.* **ingenuous** means *unsophisticated, innocent, unworldly* even to the point of being *naive.* You'll never forget which is which if you let the first <u>u</u> in **ingen<u>u</u>ous** stand for <u>u</u>nsophisticated.

irrespective / regardless

Use **irrespective** to express *neutrality, fairness, equal consideration.*
regardless suggests a sense of being *careless, indifferent,* even *reckless.*
(NOTE: There is no such word as "irregardless" — and therefore it only
seems to appear on this page. It should be reserved for humorous use.)

BUSINESSES YOU CAN START AT HOME (#86)
TEACH FLYING!

IF YOU HAVE AN AIRPLANE AND A REASONABLY LARGE BACKYARD, YOU'RE ALL SET TO GET INTO THIS EXCITING WORK! EVERYTHING YOU NEED TO KNOW IS REVEALED IN OUR BEAUTIFULLY DUPLICATED INSTRUCTION SHEET. DROP BY AND PICK ONE UP! FREE GUITAR LESSON WHILE YOU WAIT!

BILL'S CAREER CENTER & SHOE REPAIR

ALSO FRENCH WEAVING BY A NATIVE ● LET US DO YOUR LAUNDRY WHILE YOU'RE HERE

its/it's

its without the apostrophe is the *possessive* form of *it*. **it's** with the apostrophe is the *contraction* for *it is*. The apostrophe indicates the missing *i* in *is*. (NOTE: There is no such form as "*its'*.")

89

lie/lay

Present Tense	Present Participle	Past Tense	Past Participle
lie (to recline)	lying	lay	(have) lain
lay (to put)	laying	laid	(have) laid
lie (to fib)	lying	lied	(have) lied

Unfortunately, it would be wise to memorize the above.

me/myself

If I do something to myself, I use the word **myself** — as in "I hurt **myself**." If somebody else does something to me, I use **me** — as in "They gave the award to Bill and **me**" (*not* "They gave the award to Bill and myself"). Also **myself** is never a doer of anything. Never say, "Bill and myself won the award"; simply say, "Bill and I won the award."

ARE YOU IN THIS PICTURE?

From the book: *ARE YOU IN THIS BOOK?* (Based on the opera, *ARE YOU IN THIS ROOM?* from the play, *IS ANYBODY HOME?*)

principal / principle

Use **principal** to mean the *chief thing or person,* **the** *most important.* Use **principle** to refer to *rules of conduct, ethics, basic laws* behind something. Example: "The **principal** thing to remember is to base your decisions on high **principles**."

prophecy / prophesy

prophecy is the noun. **prophesy** is the verb. One must **prophesy** a **prophecy**.

THE MAN WHO COULD FLY WITH HIS TOES

From: AMAZING FEATS

raise/rise

raise means *to elevate*. **rise** means *to stand up*. Therefore, I can **rise** from a chair, and I can **raise** myself from a chair, and I can **raise** a window — but I cannot "rise" a window. It is now considered acceptable usage to "raise" children instead of "rear" children, but we should at least make sure that we really do "elevate" them.

WHY PAY SKY-HIGH! AIRLINE FARES WHEN YOU CAN...

FLY YOUR HOUSE!

WITH **WHOLE GRAIN PLUS!**

The World's Lightest Bread Dough

> As WHOLE GRAIN PLUS! Bread Dough RISES, it expands at a phenomenal rate and RAISES your house into the open blue sky above. Soon you're on your way to a dream vacation while you loaf (!) in the comfort of your own home!

But don't take our word for it! Send now for BY CUP CAKE OVER THE ANDES, the exciting true-life adventure of Bill who, with the ordinary 10-lb. steel tub of WHOLE GRAIN PLUS!, took his house and family to places they'd never been!*

Scone to Ireland!   Croissant to the Riviera!
Waffle to Washington, D.C.!
Or just popover to the next town!

FAA LICENSE
REQUIRED

Or! MAKE UP YOUR OWN RECIPES!
The sky's (wow!) the limit!

*Includes both short- and long-distance recipes.

set / sit

Use **set** to mean *to put something down*, as in "Please **set** the box on the kitchen table." Use **sit** to mean *sit down* in a chair, as in "Louella, please **sit** here." (EXCEPTION: Although it seems to *sit*, the sun *sets* — but we will not argue with the sun.)

stationary / stationery

For something that *can't be moved*, use **stationary**. For *letter writing*,
use **stationery.**

that/which

that introduces a restrictive clause or phrase. For instance, the phrase
"**that** sings" restricts the kind of horse you mean. The phrase "**that** sings"
could not be left out of the sentence without destroying its meaning. However, the non-restrictive phrase "**which** everyone knows" is not essential
to the speaker's point that "Horses cannot sing" and could be omitted.

The Eternal Conflict Between
SCIENCE AND THE COWBOY
THE HORSE THAT SINGS IS THE HORSE FOR ME!
I'M A LITTLE TEAPOT SHORT AND STOUT, TIP ME OVER AND POUR ME OUT
HORSES CANNOT SING, WHICH EVERYONE KNOWS...
...AND THEIR HUMMING ISN'T ALL THAT GREAT, EITHER
HORSE SENSE

their/there/they're

It's easy to remember that you can get from here to **there** just by adding a t. You can also remember that **they're** is *they* plus *are* with the apostrophe taking the place of <u>*a*</u> in <u>*are*</u>. What's harder to remember is that **their** means *belongs to them*. But if you remember the other two words and their meanings, you won't need to remember that **their** means *belongs to them*.

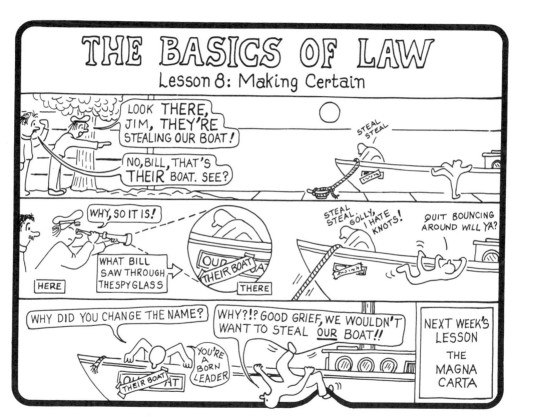

use/utilize

use is the broader word and is fine in most cases, but **utilize** has the
special sense of making use of a neglected skill or of something not
normally used for the purpose, as in "Luckily, we were able to **utilize**
the cook's knowledge of the coastline to find a safe landing place."

was / were

It's easy to confuse "if I **was**" and "if I **were**." Here's how to remember which to use: If the idea to be expressed is a possibility, use "if I **was**" ("The children asked if I **was** the king"). If the idea is known to be false, use **were** ("I said if I **were** the king I'd be wearing a much nicer hat").

111

who's / whose

who's means *who is*. The apostrophe takes the place of the missing *i*.
whose is the possessive form of *who*. Although we usually make
possessives by adding *'s* to a word (as in "the cat*'s* paw") certain
exceptions exist — like **whose** (as in "The cat, **whose** paw is in the milk,
is Felix"). (NOTE: Examples of other possessives with no apostrophes are
hers, *theirs*, and *its*.)

113

your/you're

Use plain **your** when something *belongs to* somebody, as in "I like **your** book." ("Thank you.") **you're** means *you are*. The apostrophe takes the place of the missing <u>a</u> in <u>are</u> and thus makes the contraction **you're** — as in "**You're** welcome."

THE INSIGHT OF DR. GHRUTCHAYK
from: YOU MAY NOT HAVE OSMOSIS

115

Appendix A

THE PARTS OF SPEECH

If you are among those who
have forgotten the Parts of Speech
and their functions, the following
anonymous verse that helped our
great-grandparents as children
is still of help to us:

Three little words you often see
Are ARTICLES, *a, an,* and *the.*
A NOUN's the name of anything;
As *school* or *garden, hoop* or *swing.*
ADJECTIVES tell the kind of noun;
As *great, small, pretty, white,* or *brown.*
Instead of nouns the PRONOUNS stand;
Her head, *his* face, *our* arms, *your* hand.
VERBS tell of something being done;
To *read, count, sing, laugh, jump* or *run.*
How things are done, the ADVERBS tell;
As *slowly, quickly, ill,* or *well.*
CONJUNCTIONS join the words together;
As men *and* women, wind *or* weather.
The PREPOSITION stands before
A noun, as *in* or *through* a door.
The INTERJECTION shows surprise;
As *oh!* how pretty! *ah!* how wise!
The whole are called nine parts of speech,
Which reading, writing, speaking teach.

Appendix B

A Sample List

Although not technically a usage problem, spelling variants adopted from British spelling preferences are another common source of confusion for Americans — and vice versa. While we cannot tackle the whole problem of spelling in this book, we can at least help answer another aspect of the question, "Which word should I use?" Thus, the following list as a little something extra. Add to it as you notice others.

AMERICAN	BRITISH
abridgment	abridgement
acknowledgment	acknowledgement
amuck	amok
analyze	analyse
anesthetic	anaesthetic
arbor	arbour
caliber	calibre
canceled	cancelled
carburetor	carburettor
center	centre
chiseled	chiselled
color	colour
defense	defence
enroll	enrol

AMERICAN	BRITISH
enthrall	enthral
equaled	equalled
esophagus	oesophagus
fiber	fibre
fulfill	fulfil
furor	furore
gray	grey
gypsy	gipsy
honor	honour
humor	humour
inflection	inflexion
installment	instalment
instill	instil
jeweler	jeweller
judgment	judgement
kidnaped	kidnapped
labor	labour
leveling	levelling
license	licence
luster	lustre
maneuver	manoeuvre
meager	meagre
mold	mould

AMERICAN	BRITISH
neighbor	neighbour
offense	offence
paneling	panelling
paralyze	paralyse
practice	practise (as a verb)
pretense	pretence
raccoon	racoon
sepulcher	sepulchre
shoveled	shovelled
skillful	skilful
smolder	smoulder
somber	sombre
specter	spectre
spelled	spelt
theater	theatre (also Broadway usage)
toward	towards
traveled	travelled
vapor	vapour
vise	vice (the tool)
willful	wilful
worshiped	worshipped

For more information on American vs. British spellings, see *Webster's Third New International Dictionary* (1981) pp. 21a–24a.

Bibliography

American Heritage Dictionary: Second College Edition. Boston: Houghton Mifflin
Company, 1982

    The comments on usage by the Usage Panel are extremely helpful.

Bernstein, Theodore M. *The Careful Writer: A Modern Guide to English Usage.*
New York: Atheneum, 1965

    Balanced advice and fun to read.

Fowler, H. W. *A Dictionary of Modern English Usage.* 2nd ed. revised by
Sir Ernest Gowers. Oxford: Clarendon Press, 1965

    The classic.

Strunk, W., Jr., and White, E.B. *The Elements of Style.* 3rd ed., New York:
Macmillan, 1979

    Everybody should have this book just on general principles.

*Webster's Third New International Dictionary of the English Language,
Unabridged.* Springfield, Mass.: G. & C. Merriam Co., 1981

    Has all the words anyone would need.

Index

Italicized words appear only in explanatory matter on lefthand page. Quotation marks indicate a nonstandard word.

About the Author/Illustrator

Stan Malotte is a former magazine and newspaper editor and teacher. He lives in California and writes and produces educational films.